TAKING ACTION ON CLIMATE CHANGE

DROWNING

Rising Oceans and Frequent Floods

ALEX DAVID

New York

Published in 2020 by Cavendish Square Publishing, LLC
243 5th Avenue, Suite 136, New York, NY 10016

First Edition

Website: cavendishsq.com

Library of Congress Cataloging-in-Publication Data

Names: David, Alex, 1983- author.
Title: Drowning : rising oceans and frequent floods / Alex David.
Description: New York : Cavendish Square, 2020. | Series: Taking action on climate change | Includes bibliographical references and index.
Identifiers: LCCN 2019016446 (print) | LCCN 2019980401 (ebook) |
ISBN 9781502652287 (paperback) | ISBN 9781502652294 (library binding) |
ISBN 9781502652300 (ebook)
Subjects: LCSH: Sea level--Climatic factors--Juvenile literature. |
Floods--Climatic factors--Juvenile literature. | Climatic changes--Juvenile literature.
Classification: LCC GC89 .D39 2020 (print) | LCC GC89 (ebook) | DDC 551.458--dc23
LC record available at https://lccn.loc.gov/2019016446
LC ebook record available at https://lccn.loc.gov/2019980401

Copy Editor: Nathan Heidelberger
Associate Art Director: Alan Sliwinski
Designer: Ginny Kemmerer
Production Coordinator: Karol Szymczuk
Photo Research: J8 Media

The photographs in this book are used by permission and through the courtesy of:
Cover Juergen Faelchle/Shutterstock.com; p. 4 Stan Honda/AFP/Getty Images; p. 10 NASA; p. 13 NOAA; p. 14 U.S. EPA/Wikimedia Commons/File:Trends in global average absolute sea level, 1880-2013.png/CCO; p. 16 NASA Photo/Alamy Stock Photo; pp. 18, 30, 49 ©AP Images; p. 20 Jung Yeon-Je/AFP/Getty Images; p. 24 JPL/Wikimedia Commons/File:Thermal Inertia PIA02818.jpg/CCO; p. 26 Rich Carey/Shutterstock.com; p. 27 divanov/Shutterstock.com; p. 28 ©Ian Lewis/Moment Open/Getty Images; p. 37 John S Lander/LightRocket/Getty Images; p. 38 Bloomberg/Getty Images; p. 41 Kamelia Ilieva/Shutterstock.com; p. 42 VTT Studio/Shutterstock.com; p. 47 Hughhunt/Wikimedia Commons/File:SPICE SRM overview.jpg/CC-by-sa/3.0; p. 50 By Sergio Alexander Esparza/Shutterstock.com; p. 53 VanderWolf Images/Shutterstock.com; p. 56 Romolo Tavani/Shutterstock.com.

Printed in the United States of America

Portions of this book originally appeared in *Adapting to Flooding and Rising Sea Levels* by Susan Meyer.

CONTENTS

This parking garage flooded when Hurricane Sandy hit New York City in 2012.

Introduction

New York City. More than eight million people live in this densely crowded, bustling metropolis. However, in the twenty-first century, climate change is threatening it and similar areas. The University of California, Davis, defines climate change as "significant changes in global temperature, precipitation, wind patterns and other measures of climate that occur over several decades or longer." These long-term changes affect not just climate but weather patterns as well—including how much rain and what kinds of storms a region gets. Flooding has become a big problem because of climate change. By 2100, the global sea level is expected to rise between 18 and 50 inches (46 and 127 centimeters). This would have disastrous effects on New York City, which sits near the Atlantic Ocean, and many other coastal locations around the world. The city that never sleeps may need to learn how to swim.

The Big Apple Underwater

New York City is made up of five boroughs. Many of them are only slightly above sea level. For instance, Manhattan, the most densely populated borough, is less than 16 feet (4.9 meters) above sea level. Wall Street and the Financial District are only 5 feet (1.5 m) above sea level. Because of rising sea waters, streets are in danger of becoming waterways. With the stormy Atlantic only a few feet away, this leaves New York at risk of becoming a city similar to Venice, Italy, where canals exist instead of streets and people use boats and bridges to get around the city. However, even though Venice has created an aquatic-friendly infrastructure, it still is not immune to the effects of climate change. Since 1897, the average sea level in Venice has risen 9 inches (23 cm). In 2018, water rose 5 feet (1.5 m) above normal. This was largely due to a low pressure system that came from North Africa. It brought rain and wind to Venice. Therefore, even if New York was able to use a similar approach to rising sea levels and increased rainfall, it would still not be completely resistant to the effects of climate change.

City planners in New York are not waiting until the worst happens. They are taking action now. In the part of New York called Queens, sidewalks and walkways are being elevated. Houses are being built on raised platforms. The nearby

Jamaica Bay threatens low-lying areas, and residents need to be prepared.

Some ideas regarding possible action are more radical. For instance, city developers have proposed a series of artificial islands that could be built to block sea water from reaching the city. This is called the Blue Dunes concept. The "islands" would stretch across 40 miles (64 kilometers) of coastal area between New York and New Jersey.

Increased Storms

Along with changing weather patterns come strong storms. Hurricanes are one of the strongest natural disasters that happen in the world. They seem to be getting stronger in the twenty-first century. Hurricane Sandy hit the East Coast of the United States in 2012. The 600 miles (965 km) of New York coastline were severely impacted. There was a 12-foot (3.7 m) storm surge from the ocean. This destroyed buildings and homes. It also created fires. One hundred homes burned when firefighters couldn't get to houses because streets were flooded. In New York City, forty-three people died as a result of Hurricane Sandy. Millions of gallons of water flooded the New York subway.

Many people are still suffering from the effects of the storm. Those who had insurance rebuilt their houses, but many who didn't have insurance went homeless. This affected not only people's living conditions but also things like school attendance.

In New Jersey, many students whose families lost their homes due to Hurricane Sandy stopped going to school. Their academic lives suffered because they did not have homes. Those who could rebuild their homes had to rethink the design. Many people rebuilt their homes so they would allow for flooding. They built them high off the ground to anticipate both future storms and rising sea tides.

It's not just New York City and New Jersey that are in danger of storms and flooding, but also many other parts of the Eastern shoreline. In 2018, Hurricane Florence became the wettest tropical cyclone—another name for hurricane—to hit North and South Carolina. Between 20 and 30 inches (51 to 76 cm) of rain fell across North Carolina alone. Meteorologists recorded as much as 36 inches (89 cm) of rainfall in Elizabethtown, North Carolina. The National Weather Service stated that Hurricane Florence set twenty-eight flood records. The floods were caused by both increased rainfall and rivers that overflowed. Dangerous flooding put people's lives and homes at risk. In total, Hurricane Florence caused an estimated $24 billion in damage.

The United States is not the only country at risk for these events. Parts of Asia (Osaka, Japan), Europe (The Hague in the Netherlands), Africa (Alexandria Egypt), and South America (Rio de Janeiro, Brazil) are at severe risk for flooding too. Scientists at the Geophysical Fluid Dynamics Laboratory correlate increased storms with anthropogenic, or human-caused, global warming.

Flooding as an Effect of Global Warming

Global warming warms the planet. It melts icebergs and raises ocean temperatures. In turn, this makes water expand and sea levels rise. When water has no place to go, it finds ways into the land. It floods streets and houses. It erodes shorelines. Cities become islands. Farmland becomes lakes. In March of 2019, disastrous flooding occurred in both Nebraska in the United States and Mozambique in Africa. In both areas, agriculture was affected. Flooding killed livestock and destroyed farm buildings and equipment. In both Nebraska and Mozambique, farmers were left without the land that was their livelihood.

What Can Be Done?

Flooding leaves people vulnerable and exposed. So, is anyone doing anything about this? As it turns out, all over the world, scientists, researchers, inventors, and ordinary citizens are thinking of solutions to the problem of increased flooding. They are considering many questions and exploring different technologies.

Creative solutions, advocacy, and energized hope are needed to treat the problems facing us in the twenty-first century. By changing our everyday lives, we can change our relationship to the natural world. As floods show us, we aren't separate from nature but rather part of it. It is a desperate time, but not one without hope and the means for solutions. Together, armed with information, we can prevent rising oceans and catastrophic flooding from destroying our civilization.

Greenland is shown here. This nation is home to one of the world's largest ice sheets.

CHAPTER 1

The State of Water

Over the course of Earth's long history, sea levels have continuously changed. Mostly, these have been normal fluctuations that are not influenced by outside factors. At one point, there was no ice at the North and South Poles, and the ocean was 100 feet (30 meters) higher than it is today. Now, because of climate change, the natural fluctuations are becoming exaggerated. Scientists believe these changes are unnatural and largely caused by human-produced carbon emissions.

Eustatic Changes

When scientists measure worldwide sea-level changes over long periods, they call these eustatic changes. Often these are normal fluctuations due to Earth's natural cycles. However, now, in the twenty-first century, scientists are correlating eustatic changes in sea level with human influence.

According to the Smithsonian Institution's website, the oceans account for 97 percent of Earth's water. Another 2.7 percent is frozen in glaciers. The sea level changes when this ratio of percentages changes. According to NASA, since 1993, the sea level has been rising at about 0.13 inch (3.4 millimeters) a year. There are two main reasons for this rise in sea level.

First, since the late 1800s (when the Industrial Revolution intensified), Earth's glaciers have been melting. This adds more liquid water to the oceans, making sea levels higher. Second, Earth's rising surface temperature has created thermal expansion in water. Thermal expansion is the concept that as water gets warmer, it takes up more room. This will be discussed in more detail later in the chapter. To deconstruct the reasons for these human-caused eustatic changes, an analysis of each cause is required.

Greenhouse Gases

Scientists believe that many of the outside forces that are causing sea levels to rise are the direct result of global warming caused by human activity. Most of the energy people use every day to drive their cars, power their homes, and run factories comes from the burning of carbon-based fossil fuels. This produces gases that become trapped in Earth's atmosphere. These emissions are called greenhouse gases because, like

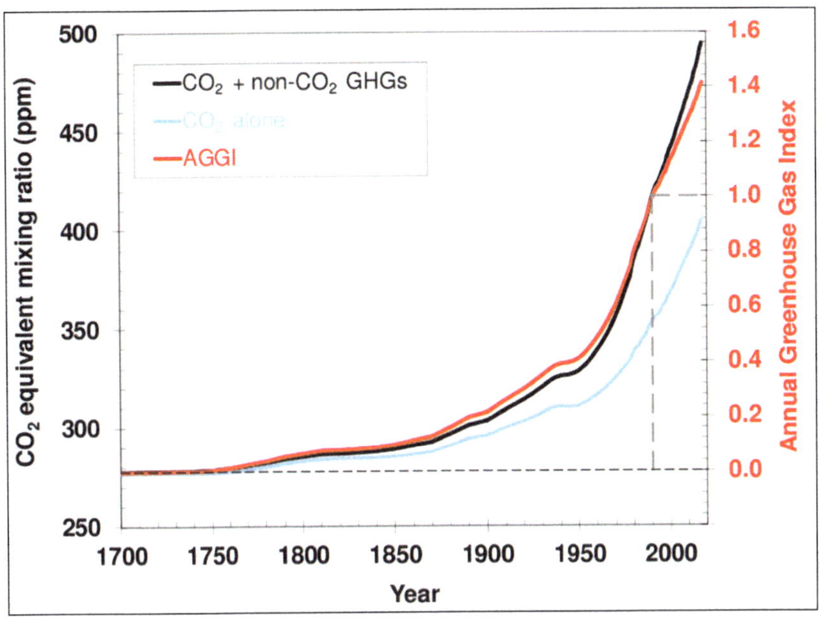

Greenhouse gas emissions increased around the time of the Industrial Revolution, as you can see in this graph.

a greenhouse trapping the sunlight's heat, carbon emissions build up in the atmosphere and prevent heat from escaping. The accumulation of greenhouse gases in the atmosphere and the resulting buildup of heat causes Earth's overall temperature to rise over time. When Earth's atmosphere heats up, ocean temperatures rise and glaciers melt.

Glaciers

Currently, glaciers and ice sheets cover about 10 to 11 percent of the world's total land area. This frozen ice is spread over 5.8 million square miles (15 million square kilometers). Not surprisingly, 90 percent of the world's ice is in Antarctica. Most of the remaining 10 percent is stored in Greenland. The largest glacier in the world is called the Lambert-Fisher Glacier in Antarctica. It is 250 miles (400 km) long and 60 miles (100 km) wide. In some points, the ice is 3 miles (4.7 km) deep. The largest glacier in the contiguous United States—the 48 states that are connected—is in Washington State. If all the glaciers in the world melted, sea levels would rise 270 feet (70 m).

The ice of glaciers is just water transformed into a solid state due to subfreezing temperatures. Therefore, when the temperature rises, ice melts and assumes a liquid state. The higher the temperature rises, the faster large ice sheets melt. Over the past century, many of the glaciers and ice sheets in both Greenland and Antarctica have lost mass. Their mass is the total measure of what they are composed of. The ice sheets and glaciers lose mass when the mass balance is negative. The mass balance is the difference between the amount of ice that is added in the winter and the amount of ice that melts away in the summer, so a negative mass balance means that

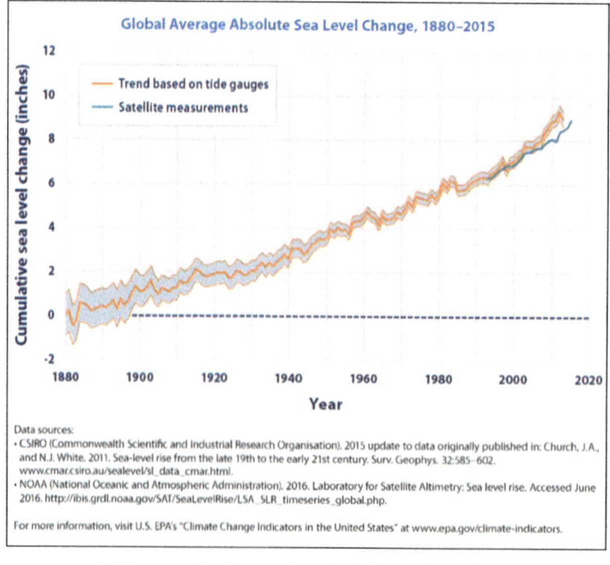

This graph shows the global sea level has increased since the 1800s.

more ice is melting than is being added during the colder months. The glaciers lose their overall mass and grow smaller as their meltwater enters the ocean.

The world's largest ice sheets are the Greenland Ice Sheet in the Northern Hemisphere and the East and West Antarctic Sheets in the Southern Hemisphere. For scientists to understand how quickly ocean levels may rise and how extensive the problem of melting ice is, they must study these ice sheets as well as smaller glaciers to see how quickly they are changing. It is important that they study both how much ice is melting and its rate of melt (how quickly it is happening).

Glaciers formed in Greenland because more snow fell than could melt, so over time, this water compressed into a large glacier. Now, these glaciers are melting. Starting in 1999, a glacier on the west coast of Greenland called Jakobshavn Glacier lost significant mass from the Greenland Ice Sheet. However, Ala Khazendar and other researchers from the Netherlands and the United States have found something unusual. Since 2016, the glacier seems to have been thickening. At first, the researchers were perplexed by this. It was still contributing to sea-level rise, but it was slowly getting thicker. Using data from NASA's Ocean Melting Greenland (OMG) mission, they determined that cold water surrounding the glacier was the cause for this change. There are water currents called the North Atlantic Oscillation (NAO) that, every twenty years, switch from being warm water to cold water. The currents had switched to

This photograph shows the Jakobshavn Glacier calving in 2012.

cold water and were helping the glacier rebuild itself. However, this thickening won't last long. Once the water switches to the warm currents, the glacier will continue to lose mass.

Thermal Expansion

Glacial melting accounts for a large part of rising sea levels, but there is another major contributor to the phenomenon. The rising temperature of Earth over time causes the existing ocean water to actually expand. How is this possible? It's actually a very simple law of physics called thermal expansion. Thermal expansion means that liquids increase in volume when they are heated. This means that the same amount of seawater will take up more space if it grows warmer.

To understand why this happens, you must understand the three states of matter. Water can exist in the world as a solid, a liquid, or a gas. When it is a gas—water vapor—it takes up much more space than when it is a liquid. When water is heated to its boiling point and becomes water vapor, it means that the molecules in water are moving farther and farther apart and taking up more space. The temperatures of the ocean waters are nowhere near the boiling point, but they are getting warmer, so the water molecules are slowly moving farther apart. The result is a greater volume of water that causes the overall sea level to rise. Rising sea levels can lead to flooding, affecting many people around the world.

Ecosystems in Danger

It is not just people who will be affected by flooding. The world also stands to lose important habitats. Wetland habitats are fragile environments that support many species of plants and animals. Approximately two-thirds of the fish that people eat worldwide depend on coastal wetlands for their survival. You may think that the rising ocean levels would actually increase the size of wetland habitats by turning existing dry land into wetlands. That is not the case, in part because people have built cities and walls along many of the coasts to prevent coastal encroachment. These urban and highly developed areas would not be able to sustain life if flooded.

If water temperatures and sea levels rise as much as expected, there will also be a loss of habitats in the Arctic and Antarctic regions. Polar bears and other wildlife depend for their survival upon the ice that is now melting. Additionally, rising sea

OYSTER-TECTURE

Kate Orff, a landscape architect, discusses her plan for the New York waterfront.

The flooding from Hurricane Sandy made people rethink how their homes were built. When rebuilding, many elevated their homes so if another storm were to hit, their basements would not flood like they had during Hurricane Sandy. Architects like Kate Orff from Columbia University began to rethink the coastline. Orff proposed a plan that would use the natural resistance of oysters to protect New York's coastline. In 2013, Orff's firm, SCAPE, submitted plans for "oyster-tecture." She proposed building a giant artificial reef that would attract oysters. The oysters would purify the water and help prevent waves from hitting New York. Orff's idea is called "Living Breakwaters" and won funding in the US Department of Housing and Urban Development's Rebuild by Design contest. The project aims both to protect the coastline of Staten Island and to improve the waters of Raritan Bay. Orff and her team show us that although disaster wreaks havoc on communities, innovative solutions can help rebuild and strengthen coastal areas.

levels can impact species that rely on low-lying habitats. Birds and sea turtles are vulnerable, as they both use coastlines to lay eggs. Populations of sea turtles are especially at risk when humans put up sea barriers, like walls on the shoreline. This destroys the sandy beaches that they use to lay eggs. Lastly, any species that live on islands are at risk. They are vulnerable to changes like rising sea levels because they may not have another place to go.

Another problem posed by rising sea levels is increased salinity (saltiness) in the world's freshwater sources. There is a limited amount of fresh water on Earth, and this water is vital to all plant, animal, and human life. Humans cannot live for very long without water, and neither can plants and animals. As salt water from the oceans rises and moves inland, it could flood rivers and freshwater reservoirs, contaminating the water we need to stay alive.

Our entire world is one large ecosystem. If one part of the ecosystem changes, all other parts respond. As sea levels rise, storms increase, glaciers melt, and water expands, floods create extensive damage to both human and animal communities. How do we anticipate how much our ecosystem is going to change? For that, we need to look to researchers and scientists around the world. Then, we need to develop ways to respond to the growing threat of floods.

The Intergovernmental Panel on Climate Change (IPCC) met in South Korea in 2018.

CHAPTER 2

Understanding and Responding to the Threat

Before humans respond to the growing threat of increased water, they need to understand the severity of the threat. Humans look to researchers and scientists, like those at the Intergovernmental Panel on Climate Change (IPCC), to understand just how much they are at risk.

The Intergovernmental Panel on Climate Change

The IPCC is warning people all over the world that temperatures are rising faster than originally anticipated. Climate conventions use the scientific work of the IPCC in understanding the risks of climate change. The IPCC plays a unique role in bringing together the scientific data from many governments in many countries. It contributes information to conventions like COP 21, where the Paris Agreement was reached. The Paris Agreement of 2015 asked participants to reduce carbon emissions to keep Earth's temperature from rising more than 3.6 degrees Fahrenheit (2 degrees Celsius) above pre-industrial levels or, more ideally, to keep the rise to below 2.7°F (1.5°C). The IPCC, after meeting for a climate convention in Incheon, South Korea, in 2018, reported that countries would have to make aggressive changes to their emissions in order to keep temperatures from rising more than 2.7°F (1.5°C). The goal for countries involved in the Paris Agreement and other climate accords is to cut emissions in half by 2030 and to reach zero emissions by 2050. If humans are not able to reduce their emissions, Earth's temperature is in danger of rising 7.2°F (4°C). According to a 2015 report by Surging Seas, a website that reports on sea-level analysis, this will cause so much flood risk it will force between 470 million and 760 million people living in coastal areas to relocate.

Accelerated Rise

According to a 2018 study conducted by lead author Steve Nerem, a professor and member of the NASA Sea Level Change Team, sea levels aren't just rising at a steady pace. Predictions from years ago are inaccurate, as sea levels are increasing at an accelerated pace.

Using European and NASA satellites, twenty-five years of data was analyzed to determine that in the 1990s, the sea was rising about 0.1 inch (2.5 mm) per year, but in 2018, that number increased to 0.13 inch (3.4 mm) per year. Nerem and his team of scientists suspect that this rate will only continue to increase. By 2100, the oceans will rise 26 inches (65 cm).

Understanding this acceleration can be challenging, as events like volcanic eruptions and climate patterns like El Niño and La Niña affect the global average sea level. Nerem and the other scientists use climate models to account for these variations. They also consult tide gauge measurement data to better understand the height of the sea, not just from satellites but from the ocean itself.

Thermal Inertia

As part of this research, scientists are looking at ways that global warming—the trigger for rising sea levels—can be slowed down. Unfortunately, global warming has already had a major impact upon the world's oceans. Reversing those negative effects will be extremely difficult and will require a long period of time. It is still imperative that scientists and ordinary citizens continue working to slow down the warming process. Damage has already been done to the oceans, even though we can't always see it with the naked eye. This is due to a process called thermal inertia.

Thermal inertia means that the warming observed in the oceans appears later than the comparable changes we see

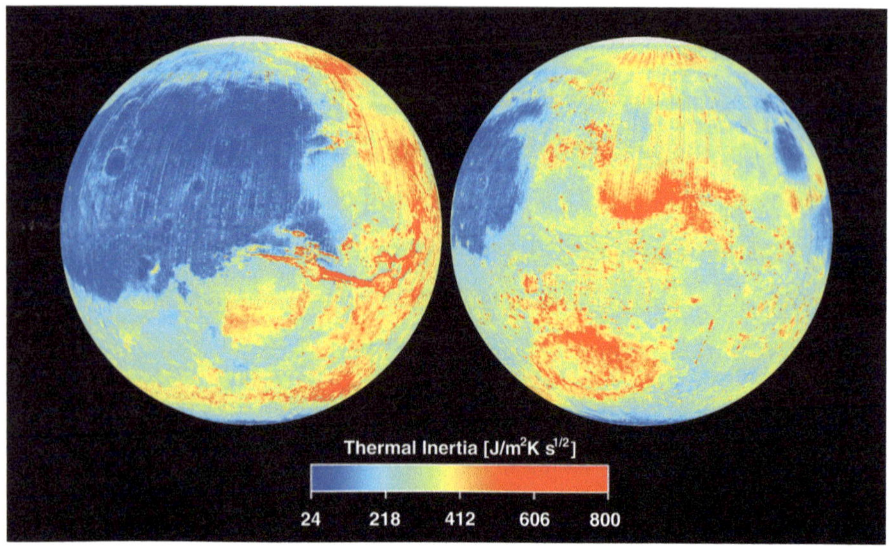

Here is a diagram of thermal inertia. Water warms and cools more slowly than air.

in air temperature. If you've ever jumped headfirst into a swimming pool, lake, or ocean in early summer, you know that even when the air is starting to get very hot, the water may still be cool for another few weeks. This is because of thermal inertia. Water warms more slowly than air, but it also holds on to the accumulated and stored heat long after the air has again cooled. So, even if global warming can be slowed or reversed, the oceans will continue to remain warmer than normal for a considerable period of time. As a result, the threat of higher sea levels and flooding will continue even if carbon emissions are slashed and global warming is somehow brought under control. It is therefore very important for scientists to come up with solutions to the threats posed by rising sea levels that, to some degree, are now inevitable.

MARINE PERMACULTURE ARRAYS

Dr. Brian von Herzen often flies his small plane, a Cessna 337 Skymaster, over the Atlantic Ocean. From his plane, Herzen can see how the Greenland Ice Sheet is melting. From 2001 to 2012, he watched puddles of ice melt turn into 6 miles (9.6 kilometers) of lakes. This is a worrying sign, but it could also create an opportunity for research and a new kind of forest.

Herzen is now trying to understand how to grow kelp forests in oceans as a way to store carbon and prevent ice sheets, like those in Greenland, from melting. He wants to repopulate ocean deserts, or parts of the ocean that have so much carbon dioxide in them that they cannot sustain life. Herzen wants to essentially re-seed the ocean's forests by putting a lattice of kelp, called a marine permaculture array, 82 feet (25 meters) below sea level. As this underwater structure receives sunlight, a trophic pyramid, or an ecosystem of other plant species, would occur: phytoplankton creates algae, more kelp, and sea grass. This would allow ecosystems to restart and carbon dioxide to get reabsorbed and pushed to the bottom parts of the ocean, which would decrease warming temperatures because less carbon would be emitted into the atmosphere.

Dr. Brian von Herzen is interested in sea grasses, like those pictured here.

Retreat, Accommodation, and Protection

There are a number of different ways humans can adapt to the challenges posed by rising sea levels. Most of these different methods of adaptation can be divided into three main categories: retreat, accommodation, and protection. Retreat is exactly what it sounds like—moving inland rather than making an attempt to stop ocean waters from encroaching on land. With a retreat strategy, the coastal zone is abandoned, and all ecosystems shift inland if possible. This choice might be made in places where trying to do anything else would come at great environmental or economic cost.

The second option is accommodation. Accommodation means accepting that sea levels will rise and salt water will move inland. Allowances are made for these changes. The coastal area is allowed to be flooded, and the area's life-forms, including humans, attempt to coexist with the changes to the environment. This option includes measures like elevating buildings so they can withstand floods, converting agricultural areas to fish farming or salt-tolerant crops, and erecting emergency flood shelters in anticipation of storm surges.

Finally, one of the most frequently employed adaptive strategies is protection. Protection means using physical barriers to prevent sea levels from encroaching on communities; existing buildings, homes, and infrastructure; and freshwater sources. These protective structures might include seawalls and dikes, but also more natural flood-control solutions like the stabilizing of dunes and vegetation in coastal areas.

This house in California is near a seawall that protects it from the water.

The appropriate response to rising sea levels depends largely on the economic and natural resources of the area in question. Different responses make sense for different environments and localities. The implementation of these three main response types will also vary. If land for a new settlement is available inland, retreat can be implemented by local, state, or national governments. The government can revise land-use regulations and change building codes so that people will no longer be able to build certain structures in at-risk areas. They will then have no choice but to build the structures they want in safer inland areas. Accommodation can be implemented, not with government action but through the innovations of scientists, architects, and inventors. Protection can be implemented mostly by the government authorities that are responsible for overseeing and guaranteeing water resources and coastal protection.

A seawall along the Isle of Wight, in England, is pictured here.

This marshland is an example of salt water moving inland.

Coastal cities around the world are wondering what an increase in flooding means for them. Property worth millions of dollars sits on vulnerable coastlines. Rising sea levels paired with greater chances of storms put many people in harm's way and at risk of losing their homes. Humans are having to both face the inevitable—that the chance for flooding is increasing—and also think of new solutions that would allow us to adapt and survive. All three responses of retreat, accommodation, and protection are being used in response to increased floods.

Villagers in Bangladesh collect drinking water after a monsoon flooded rivers and waterways in 2007.

CHAPTER 3

Innovative Solutions

As humans respond to flooding, innovative solutions emerge for confronting the increase in water. These solutions showcase how retreat, accommodation, and protection can be used in countries across the world.

Retreat in Bangladesh

One of the world's most heavily populated areas in danger of flooding because of rising sea levels is the country of Bangladesh, a small nation that borders India. Bangladesh has a large coastline, and two rivers flow through its fertile plains, where most of the nation's food is grown. These rivers, the Ganges and the Meghna, have large floodplains that, due to rising ocean levels, could effectively wipe out much of the nation's agriculture. Salty floodwaters would destroy crops and ruin soil. In addition, as many as thirty million people could be displaced by the floodwaters, and iconic animal species like the Bengal tiger could be lost. The threat to Bangladesh by global warming–induced rising floodwaters is a disaster waiting to happen for the nation's impoverished population. The country is frequently battered by tropical storms and tornadoes, which funnel along its coast and cause great destruction across the low-lying delta. As a result, the country is accustomed to regular floods. Yet the flooding is now expected to become both more frequent and more catastrophic. Sea levels along the coast are rising fast, as are water temperatures, making Bangladesh one of the most heavily populated areas in the world that is highly vulnerable to the effects of climate change.

In Bangladesh, people in coastal areas are moving whole villages inland, as their towns flood and their agriculture is threatened. In this poverty-stricken country, retreat is one of the most feasible options.

Room for the River

One example of how researchers and engineers have used the protection method of flood prevention can be found in the Netherlands. The Netherlands is a small country in central Europe. It is one of the so-called Low Countries (along with Belgium, Luxembourg, and parts of northern France and western

Germany), a territory situated in the low-lying delta of the Rhine, Scheldt, and Meuse Rivers. The use of the term "low" is apt, because half of the Netherlands lies less than 3 feet (1 m) above sea level, and one-quarter of the country actually sits below sea level.

Flooding has always been a concern for the Dutch. Since the 1500s, windmills were used to pump water off of the land. In 1993 and 1995, terrible flooding caused large-scale evacuations, and many farm animals died. The people of the Netherlands knew they had to do something. They decided to work with nature, rather than against it, and protect themselves from the floods. The organization Room for the River set goals to change thirty rivers in the Netherlands so that they would be more adaptable to flooding and increased water. In 2015, they completed many of these projects.

One project involving the Waal River required construction workers to dredge sand and gravel, relocate a dike, and create an ancillary channel so that the inland water would be able to make it to the sea quicker. The channel they created is 1 mile (3 km) long and 16 feet (5 m) deep. The newly widened river prevents the surrounding areas from getting flooded because it allows water to be collected and flow quickly out to sea.

Another project, on the IJssel River, created a large channel that would create better drainage and help preserve the agricultural functions of the surrounding areas. Again, this project allows water to get to the sea more quickly. The channel, near the city of Zwolle, is at times 5,000 feet (1,500 m) wide. When large amounts of water flow, the channel helps prevent the river from flooding and actually reduces the height of the river by about 28 inches (71 cm). The channel will probably only reduce floods once in a human lifetime. However, when not in use, it will provide space for agriculture. Additionally, this project has created more pathways for bicycles, a great means of sustainable transport and something the Dutch are famous for utilizing.

Saltwater Farms

Rising tides mean more salt water, which many people view as inhospitable to farming. However, in southern Spain, 27,000 acres (11,000 hectares) of saltwater marshlands near the Guadalquivir River are being used to grow fish. The project began in 1982. Before then, the area was once drained to raise cattle, but in 1982, developers at Veta La Palma developed a way to bring ocean water from the Atlantic Ocean into the marshlands. They then used this ocean water to create a fish and shrimp farm. Shrimp and fish species like gray mullet, sea bass, and maigre are being grown and then sold to restaurants and markets.

This seawater farm has created a new saltwater ecosystem. Algae naturally grow from the sunlight. Smaller shrimp come to eat the algae. Then, large shrimp come to eat the smaller shrimp. Fish find the larger shrimp and eat them, and then humans eat both the shrimp and the fish.

The farm has not only made the water cleaner (aquatic vegetation naturally filtrates the water) and created sustainable seafood, but in 2019, it also attracted 250 bird species, making Veta La Palma one of the largest bird sanctuaries in Europe. The developers of the project saw an increase in water not as a problem but rather as an opportunity.

Underground Drains in Tokyo

In 1992, Japan began building an engineering marvel that is protecting Japanese cities from flood damage. The "world's largest drain," or more formally, the G-Cans Project, is a series of tunnels that act as overflow drains for Tokyo. There are five cisterns that collect excess water near vulnerable floodplains. The enormous cisterns are 229 feet (70 m) high and 98 feet (30 m) wide. They are so large NASA could park a space shuttle in them. The whole project was completed in 2006 and cost about $2.6 billion.

So far, the project has been put to good use. In 2015, 670 million cubic feet (19 million cubic meters) of water fell on Tokyo because of typhoons. The engines in the part of the project called the Metropolitan Area Outer Underground Discharge Channel pumped for four days. The engines use similar technology to Boeing 737s. The project has cut the risk and damage of flooding nearly in half.

The United States is looking to projects like the G-Cans Project in Japan as a way to prevent flooding. In 1996, the city of

TIDAL ENERGY

Innovative thinkers are combining science with smart design and viewing the ocean as the new frontier of renewable energy. Ocean waves create an incredible amount of kinetic energy—80,000 terawatt-hours. One terawatt can power over thirty-three million US homes, so scientists are excited about a new technology coming from Oscilla Power, in Seattle, Washington. It's a flotation system that attaches to the ocean floor and uses magnets and rods to create electrical energy from the movement of the ocean. Although there are still questions of how to make this technology affordable, it may help harness rising ocean water for use in offsetting the climate crisis.

Houston, Texas, proposed a project of underground tunnels that would have cost $400 million to help prevent massive damage caused by flooding. The city ignored the proposal, and Hurricane Harvey hit in 2017. The tunnels would have helped alleviate the situation by draining excess water that built up in reservoirs. This shows both how countries can learn from one another and how prevention methods should not be ignored.

As seen, cooperation between countries and the sharing of information and ideas are also essential to combating increased flooding. In the context of global warming, developed countries

A cathedral-like cistern of the G-Cans Project in Japan is pictured here.

usually emit more greenhouse gases than less developed countries, but it is the less developed countries that feel the greater negative effects of rising sea levels. This is why climate conventions and global summits are essential for spreading information about flood solutions. The more we can learn from each other and think of ourselves not just as citizens of our individual countries but also as global citizens, the more we can help everyone adapt to the changing world.

In 2018, architects designed this house to withstand dangerous weather.

CHAPTER 4

A Better Tomorrow

Other solutions that utilize retreat, accommodation, and protection are being practiced all around the globe. Countries are beginning to realize that technology, architecture, and geoengineering are essential to creating solutions to the problem of flooding.

While there are a number of clever strategies currently being deployed worldwide, there are also a number of ideas that are still on the drawing board or in the research phase. All of these cutting-edge, "next-generation" ideas should be considered carefully as we continue to confront future environmental challenges and plan for the worst.

Solutions for New York City

In the introduction, the dangers posed to New York City in the event of a large storm surge were outlined. Lower Manhattan, parts of which are only a few feet above sea level, is particularly vulnerable to flooding and global warming–related rises in ocean levels. Some of the current plans being considered for the future of New York City reveal the range of possible response strategies.

Urban Planning

A number of urban planners have been tasked with coming up with solutions to potential flooding problems. One Columbia University research scientist, Klaus Jacob, believes the response to the increased likelihood of urban flooding should be a combination of retreat and accommodation. He suggests the sea-level rise may force some New Yorkers to pull back from low-lying areas. City authorities will then have to make the areas on higher ground more densely populated. They could then turn the flood-prone areas into parks and other buffer zones between the surging water and residential and commercial buildings.

According to Jacob's vision, New York City in two hundred years may come to resemble the Italian city of Venice. Venice is famous for being filled with canals that people can use to get from place to place. These canals go between the buildings like streets do in a regular city. If Jacob's proposed ideas are adopted, in the years before the ocean rises enough to spill

People get around the city of Venice, Italy, using boats on canals.

into Manhattan, dozens of skyscrapers in Lower Manhattan will have been protected in advance. Jacob proposes sealing the bases of threatened buildings and adding new entrances to higher floors. The streets of the Financial District, including the iconic Wall Street, will become canals. In this vision, which is essentially an accommodation strategy, people could take boats to get from place to place and still use the existing buildings.

Rethinking Cement

Cement may seem like a strange solution to the problem of seawater, and currently it very well might be, but researchers and developers are beginning to rethink the substance of cement.

Cement is used to create concrete, and concrete is everywhere. It is a durable, cheap substance that can be used

Concrete is used in many building designs, including this curving staircase.

to build with. Take a walk around your neighborhood, and you are sure to find examples of concrete. We use it to make homes, roofs, sidewalks, and factories.

In the twenty-first century, concrete is usually a mixture of sand, rock, water, and cement. According to science writer Paul Hawken, creating 1 ton (907 kg) of cement produces up to 1 ton (907 kg) of carbon dioxide. Per year, 4.6 billion tons (4.2 billion metric tons) of Portland cement (the most commonly used kind) are produced worldwide. This creates 5 to 6 percent of anthropogenic carbon emissions. Sixty percent of the cement industry's emissions are from a process that separates carbon from limestone to create "clinker," a component of cement.

The problem with clinker is that it is very bad for our environment. Cement is made by firing limestone and aluminosilicate clay at 2,640°F (1,448°C). This intense heat separates the limestone's calcium carbonate into calcium oxide and carbon dioxide. This carbon dioxide goes right up into the atmosphere, and as we know, this contributes to global warming.

If humans creating cement account for 5 or 6 percent of carbon emissions, we have to wonder if there is a better way. We don't want to stop using concrete, but maybe we don't need to use cement—or at least not produce it the way we have been producing it.

So, should we look to the future to think of new ways to offset this carbon? No. We should look to the past. Romans used concrete for many architectural feats, including the Pantheon. If we used today's concrete to make the Pantheon, it would have only lasted for three hundred years. With Roman concrete, it's been around for two thousand years. What did they know that we don't know? Volcanoes and seawater. The Romans used seawater in their concrete and also volcanic ash instead of cement. The ash was from a particular volcano, and it even allowed for structures to be built underwater.

Today, we don't use seawater, but why not? We have much more seawater available than fresh water, so why aren't we using it? This is a question that Lauren Kuntz, a former student at MIT, thought about ever since her freshman year when she was involved in an exciting class called Terrascope. The professor of the class gave students one question: How do you solve climate change? The students had to create their own solutions. They had very little instruction but also very few rules. Kuntz became infatuated with this question. She ended up needing more than one semester to figure out some solutions. So, she graduated from MIT and then went on to a PhD at Harvard so she could think more about possible solutions to climate change.

During Terrascope, Kuntz first started thinking about cement or cementitious materials. She and a group of other students got seawater and started figuring out how they might be able to change the way cement is used. In her 2003 master's thesis, Kuntz explains how other options besides fresh, drinkable water can be used in cement.

First, Kuntz points out that only 3 percent of Earth's water is fresh water, and we do not need to use this valuable resource to create building material. Although construction codes currently ask workers to mix potable water (water that is drinkable) in with cement, it is not actually necessary. Wastewater or brackish water (salt water mixed with fresh water) can be used instead. Kuntz also indicates that a textile material that absorbs water can be used in concrete to help reduce how much water is needed. She points out that superplasticizers (a type of polymer) can be used in cement to decrease water usage by 12 to 30 percent.

Lastly, she makes the conclusion that we can use fly ash instead of cement.

Fly ash is a by-product that results from producing iron. It is blast furnace slag (waste). Iron was an important historical building material—it was used to make New York's Empire State Building and in the Paris Métro—so today, in the twenty-first century, there is a lot of fly ash hidden in our landfills. However, although this may be a good idea in preventing carbon emissions, further research needs to be done in regards to fly ash, as it could contain toxins dangerous to human health.

Hawken is hopeful for this solution. He states, "If 9 percent of cement produced between 2020 and 2050 is a blended mix of conventional Portland cement and 45 percent fly ash, 6.7 gigatons of carbon dioxide emissions could be avoided by 2050." If we are able to use seawater, the benefits may be even higher. Therefore, this problem may be up to future scientists, like yourself, to explore: How could seawater be used instead of fresh water in our building supplies?

There is one more alternative to cement, and New York City has already started using it: crushed glass bottles. By grinding crushed glass, we not only save old soda bottles from the landfill, but we also put them to good use as building material. The fine dust of glass can be used instead of the carbon-producing "clinker."

RUSSIAN SEAWALL

In 2012, residents of Saint Petersburg, Russia, were protected from storm surges during a winter storm. How? A 15-mile (25 km) wall stretches across Neva Bay, which is in the Gulf of Finland. Saint Petersburg is sometimes called the "Venice of the North" because of its frequent floods. In the past three hundred years, the city has had more than three hundred floods. The problem with this part of the world is that stormy water from the Baltic Sea collides with the Neva River, the fourth-largest river in Europe by volume of water discharged, and creates flooding.

If the water reaches 5 feet (1.6 m), it is officially a flood. In 2019, waters had risen to 7 feet (2.1 m), which according to Russia's Hydrometeorological Center is considered dangerous.

The seawall has eleven embankments, six sluices, and two navigation channels. It is made out of steel, stone, and concrete, and cost $3.85 billion. If flooding happens, an alarm sounds, and within forty-five minutes, all floodgates are shut. Solutions like this are needed, as scientists predict that storm surges in Saint Petersburg could increase by 40 percent by 2100.

Geoengineering

Some ideas for adapting to the negative effects of climate change are more feasible than others. Some scientists and mechanical engineers think we can halt rising sea levels by reversing climate change. We can do this not by reducing our carbon-based energy use but by taking direct action to engineer our climate to best suit the needs of life on Earth. The process they suggest is commonly known as geoengineering.

The National Academy of Science defines geoengineering as a large-scale changing of our environment in order to combat the effects of changes in atmospheric chemistry. It is fair to say we are already geoengineering our world by changing the environment—for the worse—through the emission of

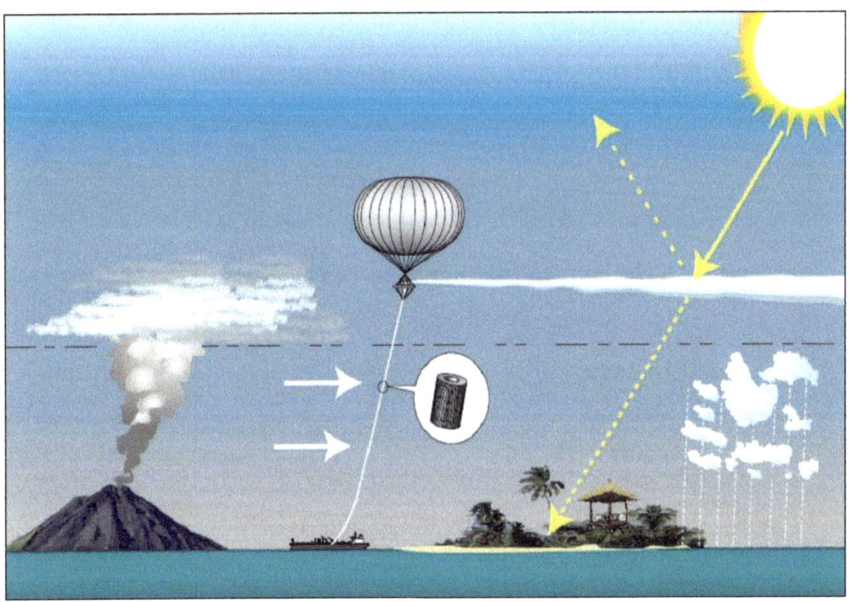

This diagram shows a type of geoengineering where scientists release particles in the air that reflect the sun's rays, thereby cooling Earth.

greenhouse gases. Therefore, some people think a solution is to try to reverse these negative warming-related changes to the environment with further human intervention. Their philosophy can be summed up as follows: we caused the problem; therefore, we should also be able to fix it.

How does geoengineering work? We know we have the power to change our climate for the worse, but do we also have the power to improve it? The most common theory of geoengineering involves compensating for the rise in global temperatures (caused by an increase in greenhouse gases) by reflecting or scattering back a fraction of the incoming sunlight, so it escapes the atmosphere instead of getting trapped in it.

Another geoengineering possibility is to reforest the United States to increase the storage of carbon in plants. Trees and plants absorb carbon dioxide as part of their normal respiration cycles. In fact, forests are considered a "carbon sink" because of their ability to absorb enormous quantities of carbon, removing it from the atmosphere. By decreasing the amount of carbon in the atmosphere, the amount of excess heat that is trapped there will also decrease. Another way to decrease carbon in the atmosphere through geoengineering is by stimulating the growth of living plants and carbon-eating bacteria in the ocean as a means of increasing the natural storage of carbon there. Oceans, like forests, are considered an important and effective carbon sink.

Workers roll out large plastic sheets that are meant to keep the snow on Germany's tallest mountain, Zugspitze, from melting during the summer.

All of these methods of geoengineering have one thing in common. They don't aim to reduce energy usage and carbon emissions. Rather, they all involve capturing and storing greenhouse gases so they cannot enter or linger in Earth's atmosphere. Many scientists are skeptical and wary of these large-scale, aggressive attempts to alter our climate because these actions may have negative consequences that we cannot yet foresee.

As shown, creative adaptations are needed to adjust to rising water levels. However, it's not just grand solutions that will change our relationship with water but also small individual efforts that we can make in our daily lives.

Houston, Texas, was flooded by Hurricane Harvey in 2017.

CHAPTER 5

Lifestyle Changes

It may feel overwhelming to learn about rising sea levels, climate change, and global warming. Floods may feel like unstoppable monsters. It may feel like either the solutions we need are far too grand for ordinary citizens or doom is only years away from happening. However, we can change the world a little bit every day by the decisions we make and the habits we practice. The way we live can also have an impact on lowering the effects of global warming.

As you have learned, global sea levels are rising for two reasons: thermal expansion and runoff from the increasing and accelerating melting of glacial ice. Both of these problems are a result of global warming, which is caused by heat-trapping greenhouse gas emissions building up in our atmosphere.

These gases are released into the atmosphere when people burn coal, oil, gasoline, natural gas, and other carbon-based fuels for energy.

Driving a car to the grocery store or purchasing items made in a factory are minor, everyday activities that require energy. In most cases, this energy is provided by a carbon-based fuel source. Almost every person on the planet uses some type of energy that produces greenhouse gases every day. Everyone is part of the problem, which means we all can be part of the solution.

Simple Steps

Each and every person can help slow and hopefully reverse global warming and climate change. There are a few simple steps that you and your family can take to reduce the amount of energy you use each day. When you leave your home, you can make an effort to use less energy when traveling from place to place. If you are in an area where it is safe to walk or ride your bike to get to school or other places you would like to go, try to use these methods of transportation instead of a car. It is also more energy-efficient to take the school bus or other public transportation in your neighborhood than to drive a car. Some places you will still need to drive to, but in those cases, encourage your family to make fewer car trips by combining errands into one big trip instead of several smaller and separate trips. You can also encourage your parents to buy a fuel-efficient hybrid or electric car to further reduce carbon emissions.

Another important way you can save energy is by saving water. It takes a lot of energy to treat the water you use every day to make it safe to drink. It takes even more energy to heat the water you use to clean yourself, your clothes, and your dishes. In fact, letting your faucet run with warm water for even five minutes uses about as much energy as it takes to power a 60-watt lightbulb for a whopping fourteen hours. As you can see, saving water is an important part of saving energy and reducing carbon emissions. You can help by turning off the water while brushing your teeth and making an effort to

An electric car sits near a charger in Amsterdam, the Netherlands, in 2011.

take shorter showers. You can also talk to your parents about installing water-efficient appliances in your home, such as low-flow plumbing fixtures, toilets, and showerheads. Another way to save water, especially hot water, is to run the dishwasher or washing machine only when it is completely full.

Using less energy is important, but equally important is where your energy comes from. Renewable energy sources like wind, solar, and tidal energy are better for the environment. When we use these sources to power our homes and schools, we avoid the carbon dioxide emissions that would have come from burning coal, oil, or natural gas. You can talk to your parents about switching to a renewable energy source. Perhaps your family can install solar panels or a solar water heater or explore green energy options with your local utility provider.

Coastlines

If you live or vacation near the shore, there are steps you can take to cause less damage to the fragile coastal environment. By maintaining the strength and health of coastlines, we make them less likely to erode in the face of rising sea levels. If we don't protect our beaches and coastlines, it will only speed up and intensify the catastrophic effects of rising sea levels and flooding.

One way you can help protect the environment while at the beach is to stay on paths, boardwalks, and designated trails when walking over sand dunes to get to the beach. These

UNCLOGGING DRAINS

As cities become increasingly at risk for floods, everyday people can take steps to make their city less susceptible to damage simply by paying attention to their drains. City drains are essential for keeping water moving. By removing sticks and leaves from your storm drain, you are creating a path for the flow of water. Additionally, consider collecting fallen debris from your yard and placing it in yard waste receptacles so that your town or city will collect it. Last, write down the number of your local sewer authority and keep it handy. Call them if you see any potential clogs in the drains in your neighborhood.

pathways are there for a reason. Using them to get to the beach instead of walking across sensitive dunes will help prevent erosion. Dunes protect the land against storm surges from the sea and also provide a home for specialized plants and animals. Human activity can threaten the existence of dunes and make the coastline more susceptible to erosion and flooding.

It is also a good idea to go only to beaches that are established for use by people. These include both public and private beaches and state parks. It is not a good idea to visit uninhabited coastlines. While it might seem nice to enjoy a deserted and secluded beach, there is probably a reason people are not allowed there. You could be having a negative impact on the health of that coastal environment.

Ambassadors of the Planet

In 2014, President Barack Obama said, "The most important title is not president or prime minister; the most important title is citizen." As a citizen, you are a steward and an ambassador of the planet. Everyday citizens are crucial to slowing global warming down, slowing rising sea levels, and preventing the risk of flood injury or damage. It's important to inform yourself about the threats that face our planet. You can spread positive change through social media, talking with friends and family, engaging in respectful discourse, and being an activist for better governmental decisions. Stay informed by reading the news and new books about climate research. The solutions that are out there may surprise you. Remember, it's small, individual actions that add up to big change. Although the threat of climate change is sizable, together we can view the challenges not as impending catastrophes but as opportunities for new lifestyles, new innovations, and new ways of thinking.

We are all ambassadors of our planet and need to protect our natural surroundings.

Glossary

anthropogenic Caused by humans.

brackish Describing water that is fresh water and salt water mixed together.

cementitious Similar to cement.

encroachment A gradual advance that presents a problem or poses a threat.

eustatic Referring to global change of sea level.

geoengineering An intentional, large-scale changing of Earth's environment by humans.

greenhouse gas A gas, such as carbon dioxide, that traps heat inside Earth's atmosphere.

mass The quantity of matter that a body contains.

mass balance The amount of mass added to something minus the amount of mass it has lost.

phytoplankton Tiny marine algae that live in the ocean.

polymer A compound or mixture.

potable Drinkable.

superplasticizer A chemical that creates flexibility when added to a material.

thermal expansion The way that matter increases in volume in response to increases in temperature.

thermal inertia Resistance to a change in temperature; a characteristic of water.

trophic pyramid A system of living plants or animals that feed off one another.

Further Information

Books

Goodell, Jeff. *The Water Will Come: Rising Seas, Sinking Cities, and the Remaking of the Civilized World*. New York, NY: Back Bay Books, 2018.

Hawken, Paul. *Drawdown: The Most Comprehensive Plan Ever Proposed to Reverse Global Warming*. New York, NY: Penguin Books, 2018.

Hofer, Charles. *Washed Away by Floods*. New York, NY: Rosen Publishing, 2018.

Machajewski, Sarah. *Storms, Floods, and Erosion*. New York, NY: Rosen Publishing, 2019.

Websites

NOAA Climate
https://www.climate.gov
NOAA Climate shows current statistics about the changing climate.

Ocean Worlds
https://www.nasa.gov/specials/ocean-worlds
This website explores the history of Earth's oceans.

Woods Hole Oceanographic Institute
http://www.whoi.edu
This site explains the newest trends in ocean research.

Organizations

Living Oceans Society
PO Box 320
Sointula, BC V0N 3E0
Canada
(250) 973-6580
Website: http://www.livingoceans.org
The Living Oceans Society has been a leader in the effort to protect Canada's coastlines since 1998. Its research into coastal ecosystems and the way that climate change affects the health of these environments is vital to future actions to protect fragile coastlines and adapt to the negative consequences of climate change and rising sea levels.

National Snow and Ice Data Center (NSIDC)
CIRES, 449 UCB
University of Colorado
Boulder, CO 80309-0449
(303) 492-6199
Website: https://nsidc.org
NSIDC is an organization operating out of the University of Colorado. It aims to distribute knowledge about Earth's frozen areas by providing tools, information, and education.

Selected Bibliography

Blackburn-Dwyer, Brandon. "Japan Could Hold the Key to Surviving Floods." Global Citizen, July 14, 2016. https://www.globalcitizen.org/en/content/japan-flood-control-superstructure-china-tokyo.

"Facts About Glaciers." National Snow and Ice Data Center. Accessed April 3, 2019. https://nsidc.org/cryosphere/glaciers/quickfacts.html.

Fecht, Sarah. "New York Is Still Feeling the Effects of Hurricane Sandy, Five Years Later." Phys.org, October 24, 2017. https://phys.org/news/2017-10-york-effects-hurricane-sandy-years.html.

FitzGerald, Emmett. "Oyster-tecture." *99% Invisible*, October 31, 2017. https://99percentinvisible.org/episode/oyster-tecture.

Hawken, Paul. *Drawdown: The Most Comprehensive Plan Ever Proposed to Reverse Global Warming*. New York, NY: Penguin Books, 2018.

"Historical Hurricane Florence, September 12-15, 2018." National Weather Service, January 10, 2019. https://www.weather.gov/mhx/Florence2018.

Klein, Caroline. *Below Sea Level: Modern Architecture & Design in the Netherlands*. Lakewood, NJ: Innovative Logistics, 2011.

Kuntz, Lauren. *The "Greening" of the Concrete Industry: Factors Contributing to Sustainable Concrete*. ME thesis, Massachusetts Institute of Technology, 2006. http://dspace.mit.edu/bitstream/handle/1721.1/34594/71252040-MIT.pdf?sequence=2.

Ocean Portal Team. "Sea Level Rise." Smithsonian Ocean, December 18, 2018. https://ocean.si.edu/through-time/ancient-seas/sea-level-rise.

"Ocean Systems." Centers for Ocean Sciences Education Excellence. Retrieved September 2011. http://cosee.umaine.edu/cfuser/resources/tr_sea_level.pdf.

OECD. *Cities and Climate Change*. Paris, France: OECD Publishing, 2010.

Pitofsky, Marina. "Historic Flooding in Italy: What Role Has Climate Change Played in the Destruction?" *USA Today*, November 1, 2018. https://www.usatoday.com/story/news/world/2018/10/31/italy-flooding-climate-change-venice/1831116002.

"Room for the Waal." Room for the River. Accessed April 3, 2019. https://www.ruimtevoorderivier.nl/room-for-the-waal.

"Sea Level." NASA Global Climate Change, September 24, 2018. https://climate.nasa.gov/vital-signs/sea-level.

Weeman, Katie, and Patrick Lynch. "New Study Finds Sea Level Rise Accelerating." NASA, February 13, 2018. https://climate.nasa.gov/news/2680/new-study-finds-sea-level-rise-accelerating.

Index

Page numbers in **boldface** refer to images.

About the Author

Alex David has her MFA from New England State College. She has written a series of books called *We the Weirdos*. Her poems and short stories have been published in literary journals such as *Green Mountains Review* and *Adelaide Literary Magazine*. Additionally, she has taught a class on eco-fiction at Canisius College in Buffalo, New York. She loves to learn and write about climate science. She is hopeful for the future.